A New True Book

BALD EAGLES

By Emilie U. Lepthien

D0124459

CHILDRENS PRESS®

CHICAGO

Bald eagle

PHOTO CREDITS

© Alan & Sandy Carey—7, 8, 9, 13 (right), 14, 17, 18, 21, 23, 25, 27 (2 photos), 28, 38, 41, 42

Journalism Services:
  © Richard Day—33
  © John Patsch—31
  © Dennis W. Trowbridge—44

Official White House Photograph—43

Root Resources:
  © Kenneth W. Fink—22, 34
  © Earl L. Kubis—10
  © Alan G. Nelson—cover
  © Stan Osolinski—4, 36 (right)

© John Running Photographs—45

Lynn Stone—2, 12, 13 (left), 36 (left), 40

To Joan Kalbacken, friend and confidant, whose faith has encouraged me.

Library of Congress Cataloging-in-Publication Data

Lepthien, Emilie U. (Emilie Utteg)
  Bald eagles / by Emilie U. Lepthien.
    p.   cm. — (A new true book)
  Includes index.
  Summary: Describes the physical characteristics, behavior, endangered status, and symbolism associated with the bald eagle.
  ISBN 0-516-01160-X
  1. Bald eagle—Juvenile literature. [1. Bald eagle. 2. Eagles.]
  I. Title.
QL696.F32L46   1989   88-38055
598'.916—dc19   CIP
                                   AC